Forgiveness
Will You
Forgive to Forget?

By Lina

PO Box 1018
Sanctuary Cove Qld 4212
Australia
Email: seek@royalpublisher.com

National Library of Australia Cataloguing-in-Publication entry

Creator: M, Lina, author.

Title: Forgiveness : will you forgive to forget? / Lina M.

Edition: 1st Edition.

ISBN: 9780994179043 (paperback)

Subjects: Forgiveness.

Description

Forgiveness is a divine gift from heaven poured into our hearts to love one another deeply and distribute kindness.

Leave the past behind to move into the future with open arms.

Dedicated to every fellow believer, who loves a pure heart and holds no grudges in his spirit.

The love for One is the love of all.

I encourage you to open up your heart and forgive one another from your core being.

Distribute love, rather than hold onto what needs to be released from the heart and benefit yourself as well as those who are listening.

Forgive in order to forget.

Remember mercy.

Guide

1	Forgive To Forget	11
2	Forgive To Love	13
3	Forgive To Succeed	15
4	Forgive To Mend	17
5	Forgive To Flourish	19
6	Forgive To Renew	21
7	Forgive To Breathe	23
8	Forgive To Rejoice	25
9	Forgive To Sleep	27
10	Forgive To Mature	29
11	Forgive To Believe	31
12	Forgive To Understand	33
13	Forgive To Enlighten	35

Guide

14	Forgive To Learn	37
15	Forgive To Release	39
16	Forgive To Soar	41
17	Forgive To Unite	43
18	Forgive To Love	45
19	Forgive To Motivate	47
20	Forgive To Rest	49
21	Forgive To Know	51
22	Forgive To Believe	53
23	Forgive To Comfort	55
24	Forgive To Receive	57
25	Forgive To Bless	59
26	Forgive To Heal	61

To You My Friends

You Are Forgiven

Forgiven

You Shall Remain Faithful

Forgive To Forget

Forgive one another as I have forgiven you, friends, that you may rest your weary soul upon my shoulders from troubled emotions that do not count.

Forgive in order to love and love to be able to forgive. I am on your side in all forgiveness.

Forgiveness is a powerful tool for every soul needing assurance in the faith of life, for this is where it all begins - in Love.

You must first forgive to be free to love yourself, God the Creator and one another.

Lift up your eyes to heaven and see where your forgiveness comes from - Me your Giver of Life.

Rescue yourself by forgiveness and move on in love.

Forgiveness is essential to you who believe in Love.

2

Forgive To Love

You are not your own, you belong to Me - your God, the Forgiver of hearts and Guiding Light. Those who ruin lives have shattered my rule of forgiveness - Love.

My Bride the Church has cried over me, but has not always submitted to me. So yield your heart to love me that you may be forgiven of pointing of the finger and false accusations. As tender and loving, as strong and firm I am - realistic and sure, confident and assured.

Rule over the world by obeying my Will, lest you lose yourself in spirit and wander about like a lost sheep without a Shepherd - a lost soul without a Master.

Keep calm during the stormy weather and be at peace by the love you have inside.

I am watching and waiting for your response. Compromise not the rule of faith to forgive.

3

Forgive To Succeed

Disturb not my presence by your unforgiveness of today.

Rule over your heart to forgive, lest you become disturbed by trouble.

"Be not fooled and give not into temptation, for it is not of me," says your Maker.

The fowler shall not disturb your heart a second time around with unforgiveness, for you have learned the lessons necessary.

I, your God, shall restore double to you, as you forgive your brother, sister and all those who have sinned against you.

I shall acknowledge you before all men, as you forgive all those who have done you wrong and spoke evil against you.

Forgive as I have forgiven you and you shall be restored back to health.

4

Forgive To Mend

The rule of forgiveness is love, just as the rule of love is forgiveness. I shall watch you grow in my presence of love and tend to you carefully.

Forgive lest you forget your identity-- of who you really are in me, for I am He, who forgives all your sins and transgressions.

Forgive lest you forget my support of love - The truth spoken in love.

Indulge in forgiveness and be awakened by love, mercy and grace supporting you.

I am your honor of praise and Ruler over your heart, if you would allow me.

Consecrate yourself through my Word of forgiveness and submit to me wholeheartedly.

I created you and re-created you, formed you and reshaped you to dwell in my forgiveness of security. So forgive, for it is my rule of Love.

5

Forgive To Flourish

Trust not your own mind when it tells you: "Forgive not," but lean on my wisdom and understanding instead, to show you the Way of forgiveness through Love.

You are not on your own in all these trials and tribulations, for I have called you 'Faithful,' and faithful you shall remain strong and steadfast in love, in order to continue forgiving the wrong that people commit against you.

Do not wrong anyone nor even hold a grudge against yourself, for I am your beginning till the very end.

Forgive and you will find favor resting upon your shoulder. So, release to be released.

Hold hands with forgiveness and work against unforgiveness leading you astray on the wrong path of sorrow. Indulge yourself in my forgiveness through love.

6

Forgive To Renew

As you forgive, trouble shall flee and not cease you a second time around. So burden not yourself with the fire of entanglements endangering your soul, body and mind. Be assured of faith working through your own heart of forgiveness.

The Power of Love Rests on Forgiveness.

You are empowered to set the captives free - lavish them by forgiveness, that they may be set free to be healed and soar the mountaintop to an incredible height.

Direct your footsteps on towards forgiveness that you may fall in love and be lifted up in glory. Lavish yourself with forgiveness and restore the times lost through unforgiveness.

I have empowered you to walk the walk, not just to talk the talk of love. Amen?

Aim higher, child, for you are forgiven.

7

Forgive To Breathe

Forgive and live not in regret. Time is coming to an end for all, and a new beginning has just begun.

I shall restore you back to health as you forgive, for I am the Forgiver of hearts. I seek pure intentions - neglect me not. Neglect not your gift of love to forgive.

He who loves you has set you free and unshackled you from your own prison walls through forgiveness, that you may live a life of freedom - Free from any restriction and unforgiveness opposing you. You shall lack nothing as you forgive.

Unforgiveness is a curse not to be tampered with. Engage not with unforgiveness while you have forgiveness running through your veins. Remain pure from all entanglement and be locked in firmly with forgiveness, so that you may not be ensnared by unforgiveness.

8

Forgive To Rejoice

The pure essence of love is found in total forgiveness.

You are revealed by your true colors of love through forgiveness, so forgive to reveal the purity of your heart.

I am one with you in spirit, but now forgive from the heart, that your soul may prosper in the areas of love.

Forgive as the power of forgiveness enlightens your soul to be merciful.

I am on my way to you. Live in peace with yourself, for you have proved faithful.

I have chosen to forgive all your transgressions; now it is your turn... go and do likewise.

Choose to forgive, for the time has come to a final stage. Everything is about to be renewed, so forgive lest you live in regret to no return.

9

Forgive To Sleep

You are anxious and have no energy to even consider why-- the reason is that you need to forgive in order to forget and regain strength.

The power of love comes from forgiveness. Be not entangled by trouble, rather escape the grip of the enemy by forgiving here and now.

Be not moved by trouble and say to yourself, "I shall never forgive you for this or that," instead say, "You are forgiven for all the wrong you have done to me, as well as to yourself; may Heaven judge between me and you."

I am to be honored, yes, but forgiveness is meant to be given not just spoken. You were called to forgive, and forgive you shall. Forgive to be forgiven. Release yourself by forgiving those who have wronged, you and be set free from the snare imposed upon you. You are not to judge but to love in order to forgive, and forgive in order to grow in love.

10

Forgive To Mature

I shall no longer pamper you, O child of mine. If you do not forgive those who have sinned against you, as well as yourself, you shall not be free from the burdens that may come upon you. So be free from these memories of the past and move on forward... step at a time.

Burden not yourself with the troubles of this world burdening you with unforgiveness. Forgive and let go of these past thoughts that hold you back, for I am your Peace during time of war. I have taught you to forgive. Hold not on to unforgiveness, lest you be burdened by trouble and reject the truth shown you.

You are mine; now move in that direction - on that highway of forgiveness, so that you may not slip along the way and lose your foothold.

I have forgiven you, now you too, forgive and be free from all these burdens entangling your thoughts.

11

Forgive To Believe

I am your Giver of life not death. Walk in the path of forgiveness that we may meet along the way of love and be showered with my eternal blessings.

I have given you enough time to think about what is best for you. Forgive, O my child, and you shall not live in regret.

Kill and die by unforgiveness, or choose to live in forgiveness and release others into a spacious place - The Heavenly Room of Love.

I am your All and have forgiven you. How much more should you forgive as a child of the Most High God of Love. Your Forgiver has spoken... now move with Him in forgiveness and be showered in praise.

I am here to watch you grow in love, faith, and hope through forgiveness. Your journey of love is not yet over, so forgive.

12

Forgive To Understand

He who loves you has set you free to live a life of forgiveness.

Forgive lest you be burdened by trouble and be tempted by your enemy, the evil one, who seeks to entrap your spirit-- robbing your soul by entangling your mind with corruptive thoughts. Defiled he is; do not give into his ways. He will rule over your heart if you are not careful, and will lead you astray if you are not aware of his evil schemes. You are not to pamper him nor indulge him with thoughts that are not of my good. Look to Me - Your Guide in all matters.

You are free to choose the path of love and forgiveness or the dreary way of unforgiveness and fall off the cliff from the highway of righteousness. Rule over your mind by my spirit ruling over you.

Be self-controlled to be able to forgive. Amen?

13

Forgive To Enlighten

Am I the one you are forgiving when you forgive your brother? Are you not forgiving yourself when you forgive others.

The future is purposeful, so forgive quickly before the day is over and the night falls.

I shall listen to your heart cry and to your plea as you ask me to forgive those who have sinned against you, that you may be restored to your rightful place in me.

I am the Alpha and the Omega, and my power of love and forgiveness is living in you.

Your new journey shall not restrict you. Be empowered, you are not restricted.

I have empowered you to walk with me the walk of forgiveness while speaking truth to the nations. Serve me wholeheartedly and you will grow stronger in love.

14

Forgive To Learn

Enlighten your soul by forgiveness and be showered in Love.

I am your Anchor of hope, therefore, forgive to find me present.

The power is in your hands to forgive and you must do so. O child of Love, choose to release yourself from this burden of unforgiveness holding you back from me. Forgive to forget and shine in my glory.

Be awakened by mercy sustaining you. I am your Anchor of forgiveness. Be entangled not by unforgiveness.

Forgive lest you remember the trouble caused by unforgiveness.

Leave the old ways behind and look forward towards a new start - A new beginning.

Your eternity begins when you forgive.

15

Forgive To Release

Enlightening words should always be your number one priority of forgiveness, spoken from the heart of love. Your sure foundation is me living inside your heart of love and forgiveness.

Enlarge the place of your forgiveness and be not a burden to yourself. I am on your side. Now help your brother forgive all the wrong you have done to him.

Keep climbing those walls of love by the power of forgiveness. Through forgiveness, your journey becomes complete and enlightened to carry you through in love.

Stimulate your thoughts with wholesome thinking, O my child, for you are released to roam as you please in my Kingdom of love with freedom through forgiveness.

Cower not under unforgiveness, just forgive.

16

Forgive To Soar

The pain flees when you forgive, O beloved. So free yourself like a gazelle from the hand of the entrapper by forgiveness without holding on to hard feelings.

Be not entrapped by unforgiveness. Instead, cry out to me from the heart for release, and I will restore twice as much to you.

I do not choose to say one thing and act on another, therefore, nor should you. Forgive and forget, lest you neglect the gift of Love.

I love you gracefully with an undying love of my mercy of grace and forgiveness.

You are to let go and allow forgiveness rule over your heart. You are mine, therefore forgive. Your future is clear - pass through.

Undress yourself from unforgiveness and clothe yourself with the garment of forgiveness in love, that you may benefit twice.

17

Forgive To Unite

Empower positive thoughts and encourage forgiveness to receive enlightening ideas.

Be creative in your mission of forgiveness and see it from the right angle - not from the rear vision of disregard, but with a direct approach. Approach forgiveness in Love, and Love will forgive you.

Forgive and let go, O child. Forgive and you will not be burdened by trouble. Unforgiveness is a burden drowning in sorrow.

Be free that you may be released to fly without any setbacks holding you from soaring on the mountaintop. Soar on the wings of love and be free from unforgiveness, by the power of forgiveness. Follow the Light of Life.

The future is not dim, but bright if you are living in forgiveness. You are now free to soar on high, above the clouds of unforgiveness.

18

Forgive To Love

Forgive, lest you be bound by trouble from the heart and release bad vibes, for everyone desires to be loved and come to know who they really are by forgiveness.

Live a life of pleasure through forgiveness that you may inherit a blessing and be one with your soul as one truly faithful.

Acknowledge faith and faith will reward you, for without faith we cannot please God, for it is only through faith, that one can truly be faithful, loyal and forgive from the heart of love in action.

I am on your side. Turn not away from me, when I speak, for I lead you in way of truth, love and forgiveness - The highway to heavenly places.

Remember to forgive, no matter the cost, for you are an overcomer and nothing shall hold you back from forgiving.

19

Forgive To Motivate

Demonstrate justice by love and come to acknowledge the truth by forgiveness, for I am with you in spirit, and will enlarge your heart to forgive as you focus on your true identity in love.

I am with you when you forgive, for the demons of darkness have no power over you, nor can overshadow your view once you have been forgiven to forgive. So, let go and forgive, for I am teaching you the way to love.

Love to forgive and forgive to be able to love.

The future is open for you, be released and continue to forgive through love, and I am with you heart and soul.

Lead the way to the everlasting through forgiveness and be lenient in your approach towards forgiveness. Lean on me, for I am your example of forgiveness. Your Guide is in control of your heart.

20

Forgive To Rest

Compromise not your faith by unforgiveness, for time is now short not to be able to forgive. Forgive you must, for the sake of the soundness and privilege of your mind.

Inherit a blessing through forgiveness and lead the way of love towards salvation. No one can inherit peace unless they forgive from the heart and let it go by the spirit of love, supported by grace.

I, Forgiveness, am knocking on the door of your heart; hear my call and forgive, lest you become an arrow in the enemy's hand and a target for him to destroy by manipulation, grief and sorrow. Resist his attempts by forgiving one another in love, mercy and grace.

Help yourself by forgiving, for your future is bright and does not deserve complications by any form of sadness, retaliation or grief. So forgive and let go, to be sound in mind and released in spirit.

21

Forgive To Know

Be free from unforgiveness and lean towards forgiveness, for your future depends on it. Be covered by forgiveness, lest you walk alone upon the earth and neglect to find yourself through forgiveness. The power is in your hands not to suffer, but to proclaim a place for yourself through having a forgiving heart.

Conquer death by giving forgiveness a chance to live and breathe in your veins through the love and mercy given you, supported by grace.

Love as if there is no tomorrow, and forgive as if you only have today.

Forgiveness is essential in your life, just as love is, and can only become complete and united through forgiveness from the heart of love in action. You too, forgive, that you may prosper by the love you share with one another.

Let go of past difficulties, which unforgiveness caused and live in peace with one another.

22

Forgive To Believe

Reflect on what I am saying: Forgiveness is a reflection of your soul, released by the spirit of love. So, forgive lest you forget your roots and become a wander upon the earth with nowhere to turn.

Forgiveness is a vital part of your life-- releasing your mind from agony and sorrow. So forgive lest you forget who you are and become disturbed by agony of soul and spirit.

Reflect on what I am saying: For your heart is crying out to forgive and your spirit is yearning to be released. Forgive lest you remember the agony of past sorrows and become injured with no one to help or support you.

Keep calm, for the waters have reached your neck. Let go, so that you may hear the voice within you more clearly, crying out, "Forgive and let me take over your burdens, for I am with you to help you let go, and let go you must".

23

Forgive To Comfort

Be no longer a slave to your own burden of unforgiveness and release love through forgiveness.

I will call upon my angels and they will support you by grace, for you are not alone in all this, but I am with you on all levels.

Help yourself forgive, that I may increase your territory, and give you a place of pleasure, rather than remaining in a place of wailing, released by unforgiveness.

Forgive that you may move mountains and never look back to your own sorrows of corruption and grief.

Forgiveness is your release and only way out; so have mercy on yourself and forgive.

Become one with your spirit and rest in love, that you may grow strong, and no longer be terrified by trouble or any form of disturbance.

24

Forgive To Receive

Illuminate your life with gladness and your days with pleasure by your forgiveness released and let go of past trouble that unforgiveness caused.

Help one another forgive from the heart, for there is no burden too greater nor sorrow ever too big, that forgiveness cannot release.

Be one with your spirit as you forgive, and release love in motion by the forgiveness you share with one another.

The key is in your hands; you can turn it as you please, for you are in control of your own destiny once you let it go and free yourself by forgiveness releasing you in action.

Demonstrate love in action and you will grow strong in spirit, for your life depends on the choices you make.

He who loves you is here to support you.

25

Forgive To Bless

Once you are here, do not let go. Forgive and be free, for forgiveness is a burden that must not be carried around.

Enjoy the pleasure of life, by releasing yourself from the ache and pain of unforgiveness, and delight yourself with love through forgiveness.

Be one with your spirit and ache no more, for you have accomplished success-- once you forgive.

The journey is no longer corrupt, but smooth riding from here on, for you have walked in the direction of love, mercy and grace.

You have achieved much and now you have found favor with forgiveness yourself.

Bravo; mission accomplished and completed by the spirit of grace beholding you in love.

I am on your side and will never let you go.

26

Forgive To Heal

Forgiveness is a key to freedom.

Forgiveness is a very powerful weapon stored up against the enemy. It shatters his eyes and keeps him blinded by the glory covering you from sight.

Forgiveness shall restore you back to health, enlighten your way, bring you prosperity and raise you up to a higher level in love.

Forgive lest you forget who you are - merciful. Forgive to forget the old and move with the new. You shall be renewed without reservation.

Acknowledge faith and forgiveness shall reward you.

You are a lover of Life... so live life in full through forgiveness and enjoy prosperity.

Keep your head up and forgive from the heart. Your future of restoration draws near.

A Prayer

From The Heart

Forgive Me

Oh, God, forgive me, that I may learn and be One with you in spirit. I need your touch upon my life that I may walk in your Kingdom as one truly faithful and loyal to your truth of love and forgiveness.

Help me forgive from the heart, that I may be submissive to your truth, and love as you have loved by forgiving us.

Lead us the way of truth in your love, that we may be covered by grace all the days of our lives. May we learn how to be one with you in spirit and with one another, for without you, we are lost sheep, who can easily be led astray by the enemy, who has no mercy. But by your love we are protected from any damage that he may cause by binding us to his unforgiveness.

I commit my heart, soul and spirit to you, and lead others to know the Way of forgiveness, which leads to heavenly places and leaves no sorrow, grief of regret.

Help Me Forgive

Oh, God forgive me, I pray, and help me forgive, that I may be forgiven, for I need you in my life and desire to live your life of love and forgiveness. You are the One I honor and long to please all the days of my life, so help me forgive, that I may understand Love and walk in all your ways of goodness.

Help me be One with you in honor and grace, that I may love as you love and forgive as you forgive.

My heart says to forgive sometimes, but my head plays up on me and I don't know what to do since the hurt is so deep. So, help me understand, that I may know your ways, and walk in your truth all the days of my life, without any form of restriction caused by unforgiveness-- killing the soul, destroying the spirit of love.

Thank you for loving me and taking me unto yourself.

Forgiven

Forgiven, I stand strong and forgive all those who hurt me, for I am a conqueror and a warrior of love. Therefore, I shall forgive and not fear what man can do to me.

I uphold the cause of love and unite myself to heaven's throne-- by loving one another in the midst of this darkness surrounding us.

I give my life freely to forgiveness and will not abort it to unforgiveness.

I yield my heart to love and submit my spirit to your call of authority in the making of perfection through forgiveness.

I love to do good, and will not surrender my heart to anything that would steal or rob me from my authority to give out love and honoring forgiveness setting me free.

Enjoy forgiveness and lets forget unforgiveness.

Run with love on your side.

Love One Another As You Forgive
Be Released

★

Mat 6:14 **For if you forgive other people when they sin against you, your heavenly Father will also forgive you.**

Joh 20:23 **If you forgive anyone's sins, their sins are forgiven; if you do not forgive them, they are not forgiven.**

Mat 6:15 **But if you do not forgive others their sins, your Father will not forgive your sins.**

> # Perfect Yourself In Love To Forgive
> ## *Be Blessed*

★

1 Jn 2:12 am writing to you, dear children, because your sins have been forgiven on account of his name.

1 Jn 1:9 If we confess our sins, he is faithful and just and will forgive us our sins and purify us from all unrighteousness.

Heb 8:12 "For I will forgive their wickedness and will remember their sins no more."

A NEW BEGINNING

A NEW JOURNEY

Check out our range of exciting and motivational new **B**eyond **W**oman® books, inspirational music, irresistible fragrance and selection of empowering products!

facebook.com/AuthorLinaM
facebook.com/BeyondWoman
facebook.com/MyBeyondWoman
twitter.com/MyBeyondWoman
instagram.com/MyBeyondWoman
youtube.com/MyBeyondWoman
www.MyBeyondWoman.com

www.ingramcontent.com/pod-product-compliance
Lightning Source LLC
Chambersburg PA
CBHW052131010526
44113CB00034B/1860